# Thrifty Girl

# KICK$ YOUR FINANCIAL BUTT

*get a grip on your finances without dying of boredom*

Thrifty Girl, Inc.
4343 North Clarendon Avenue, #1501
Chicago, Illinois 60613
www.thriftygirl.net

ISBN-10: 0-978-83570-0
ISBN-13: 978-0-978-83570-0

First Edition 2006

Design, photography and illustrations by Alexis Steinkamp

*For Nanny and Aunt Mary*
*You taught me the value of a quarter. I will always be grateful.*

## SPECIAL THANKS TO...

Stacey Bashara, who dubbed me *Thrifty Girl*, insisted that I write this damn book and backed it up with thorough editing. Lisa Manzari, who smacked my ramblings into high gear, repeatedly. Jeff Libman, who believed in *Thrifty Girl* and never let up. Randy Stearns, who kept things in perspective.

My sister Sarah, *Frugal Girl*, who inspired and tolerated me through the entire journey. Mom, who made numerous suggestions. Dad, who promised I would learn to write when I had something to say.

And finally, thanks to the multitude of friends, family, virtual stangers and one ex-agent who kept *Thrifty Girl* moving forward.

# CONTENTS

INTRO Talk is Cheap  1

CHAPTER 1 Quit Bitching  3

CHAPTER 2 Commence Counting  7

CHAPTER 3 Where the Hell?  11

CHAPTER 4 Dig Yourself Out  21

CHAPTER 5 Time is Your Slave  30

CHAPTER 6 Steer Clear of Total Disaster  35

CHAPTER 7 Kick Every Stone  40

CHAPTER 8 Thrifty Forever  46

# THRIFTY GIRL'S WARNING

Like a bottle of Robitussin, a box of condoms or a shot of Botox, this book comes with a warning. This little book will change your life. Consider yourself warned. If, however, you are completely and utterly set in your ways, DON'T BOTHER WITH THIS BOOK! You're wasting your time. Put it down right now! Give it to a friend, drop it off at the library or start a fire.

# TALK IS CHEAP

Face it, you have a problem. Your finances are a mess. You wouldn't be reading this book if they weren't. Roll up your sleeves and let's get to the bottom of it. You don't really have a clue about your current financial situation, do you? It's OK. You're not alone. *Thrifty Girl's* message to you is: *Get a grip!*

The cure for this nasty condition is simple. Light a fire under your ass and become a thrifty girl! In today's world, being thrifty isn't about being cheap, stingy or boring. Thrifty is being smart, sensible, and shrewd with your dough. Stop being a slave to spending, a victim of plastic and blinded by a self-destructive path to mass consumption. Need a translation? Stop buying loads of crap, girl! Start thinking about what YOU want from life, set goals and get moving.

I speak from experience. I was in a mess of a financial situation once. In my 20s, I was a starving artist who lived from paycheck to paycheck. Sure, I lived in a cool loft space with exposed brick. But I worked a hundred crappy jobs. I even cleaned houses and jockeyed espresso. I did what I referred to as "a little bit of this and a little bit of that," and I was honestly just scraping by. I was always scrounging around for my next gig. I was miserable. I was broke. And I was totally trapped.

So, how did I break free? One day, I ran into this really gorgeous guy shopping at Barneys. I caught him admiring my Moschino bag. As it turns out, not only was he a stunning specimen, he was loaded — house-in-Paris loaded.

Girls, dream on! Any guy who admires your bag is gay. And no queen in Barneys is going to save your royal hide.

OK, so how did I REALLY break free? Simple: I learned to be thrifty. It totally turned my life around. Today I keep my expenses low by being thrifty — not cheap — just smart with the green. Every time I do something particularly thrifty, my friend Stacey says, "For god's sake, girl — will you write that freakin' book? You can squeeze blood from a nickel!"

# 1

# QUIT BITCHING

That's right. Quit bitching about your financial situation! You're not a rag doll. You're a powerhouse. Aim high and plan to conquer! You have what it takes. If you didn't, you'd still be drinking strawberry wine coolers.

It's high time to get your head out of the sand and start thinking about the things that really matter to YOU. Do you want to get out of debt, change careers, start a non-profit organization, buy a condo, adopt a child or travel? Make a list. Together we'll figure out what it will cost. Don't worry that it seems like it's going to take a village to make your dreams come true. Just dream. We'll sort out the tedious details in due time.

**Doesn't this light a fire under your ass?**
I know a girl who saved up, quit her job and traveled around the world for a year. I know another girl who saved up and bought a house. I know girls who saved up and went back to school, girls who started a business and one who had a child by herself. How? They used their BRAINS. They had a goal, made a plan and stuck to it. You can do this, too! *Thrifty Girl* is here to show you how.

**Get balanced**
When was the last time you actually balanced your checkbook? You know… check number, date, description, amount and THEN ACTUALLY BALANCED your checkbook. I know it's the very last thing you're thinking about Friday night when you grab 80 bucks from an ATM. Just do it!

**Net savings**
*Pain and suffering:* Those bounced check fees could send a child to college.

**Take advantage**
If your place of employment offers a tax-deferred 401(k) retirement plan, drop everything and take advantage of it! You won't miss the money from your pay check as much as you might think. And, if you start making contributions early, you may actually be able to retire. Or you could work like a dog 'til you drop dead at 68. Your choice.

**Net savings**
*Abandonment:* When your friends decide to retire to Cabo San Lucas, you can join the parade.

**Short-term goals** *so you don't go nuts*
I know what you're thinking—I'm going to make you live like a hermit in a refrigerator box under a bridge so you can save up enough money for this crazy dream thing. I certainly didn't do that, and I don't expect you to. What were some of my short-term goals? I wanted to put together a portfolio to get a better job ($100), fly home for my sister's graduation ($220) and take a Spanish class ($99). Brainstorm below.

| GOAL | COST |
|------|------|
| | ( ) |
| | ( ) |
| | ( ) |
| | ( ) |
| | ( ) |
| | ( ) |

**Long-term goals** *so you actually have A FUTURE*
I'll tell you what my goals were—land a job I loved, buy a condo ($3,000 down payment—that was 10 years ago), travel somewhere new every year ($1,000/yr), be semi-retired by 40 (I'm still working on this one, but I have a few more years) and never retire. I like to keep busy. I'd probably become a fat, lazy Food Network junkie if left to full retirement. This is your chance to dream. If you have credit card debt, getting out of debt should be a top priority. Think big. Brainstorm below.

| GOAL | COST |
|------|------|
| | ( ) |
| | ( ) |
| | ( ) |
| | ( ) |
| | ( ) |
| | ( ) |

**Start your emergency fund** *and save for a rainy day*
Don't even start with, "I don't need an emergency fund."
You need one. Everyone needs one. Why? 'Cuz shit happens and you don't want to end up homeless, bankrupt, sleeping on you ex's sofa, living with your parents or living with your in-laws. In a word—SCREWED. You get the idea? Start saving something today. You'll be amazed how fast it adds up.

How much do you need in your emergency fund? I recommend six months of basic expenses—rent or mortgage, utilities, food, insurance, car payment, gas and minimum credit card payments. Figure out your expenses for a month. If your monthly expenses are $2,000, you need six times that, $12,000.

| EXPENSE | COST PER MONTH |
| --- | --- |
| | |
| | |
| | |
| | |
| | |
| | |
| | |
| | |
| | |
| | |

**TOTAL MONTHLY EXPENSES** ⟶

Write the monthly total in the first blank below and multiply by 6 for the fund total. Make a note below.

Go ahead and calculate!

$ _____ per month X 6 months = $ _____

♦ THRIFTY TIPS ♦

**Saving on necessities**
You probably buy the same stuff week in, week out—the same toothpaste, the same hair gel and the same frozen entrée. When these non-perishable items go on sale, don't hesitate, stock up!
**Net savings**
*Shopping boredom:* Buy-one-get-one-free is as exciting as a stock boy in leather pants.

**Quit and feel fabulous**
Stuffing your face with crappy, cardiac-arrest-inducing entrees and desserts? Smoking even when it's not after sex? Dying your hair with nasty chemicals? Are you trying to kill yourself? That's what it looks like from here! Why not quit? Give your body a rest. You'll feel better and you might even live longer!
**Net savings**
*Extra fat:* Have you seen *Supersize Me*?
*The taste of food:* Everything tastes better when you quit smoking.
*Pain and suffering:* You won't have to lay on your bed to zip your "fat" jeans.

# ✦ THRIFTY TIPS ✦

## Where's the money?

Not every girl out there is making 76¢ to a man's dollar. If you choose the right profession, you can knee those boys in the crotch. For the same time in the educational system, you could be a social worker making $22,000, an elementary teacher making $32,000, or a nurse making $48,000. Don't waste your precious time crying about the 76¢ thing. Get skills that pay.

**Net savings**

*Whining:* You'll be laughing all the way to the bank.

## Avoid shipping

There's nothing more annoying than spending $25 to send a $25 gift. It doesn't make sense! What do I do? I avoid shipping. I send a card with a check or a gift card. Think about it. For the cost of the gift and shipping, I could send a card with a $50 check and never have to leave the house. I live in Chicago, that's something to consider at least nine months of the frigid year.

**Net savings**

*Frostbite:* My post office is an eight-block trek.

Brilliant ideas. Calculations. Notes.

---

### Chapter 1 homework: 2-30 minutes

Start your emergency savings fund today. I don't care if it's 50¢ in a Mason jar or 100 bucks in a savings account. Start it today. I think it's a good idea to have a special account, but it's not mandatory. If things are really tight and you're going the way of the Mason jar, open an account after you've accumulated enough savings to earn interest. Most savings accounts have a $100 minimum balance. While you're at the bank (or on the phone/internet), you may want to consider a monthly automatic transfer from your checking account to keep your emergency savings fund upwardly mobile. Keep track of your balance on page 48 under *savings*.

☐ Homework complete!

# COMMENCE COUNTING

So, you have some cash in your pocket and some in a checking or savings account — maybe both. Great, how much? Do you have a secret piggy bank, a $100 savings bond, a 401(k) or Roth IRA? What's it all worth? What's liquid? When can you get your hands on it?

Remember when you were a kid trying to make it look like you didn't have much food left on your plate? Remember spreading it around or hiding it under your fork or behind a glass or feeding it to the dog? Well, that was cute when you weren't paying rent. Now it's time to grow up. It's outright dangerous to play this game with your money — your future is watching. Pile it up and let's start counting.

**Appreciate vs. depreciate**
When you go shopping,
you should always consider
whether your object of desire
will appreciate or depreciate.
Real estate usually increases in
value. Most things, from your
iPod to those fancy boots, lose
value the second they're off
the rack or out of the box. A
new car loses around a quarter
of its value in the first year.
Try to avoid spending gobs of
cash on items that will depreciate. What's the best way to
avoid losing to depreciation?
Buy used!

**Net savings**
*Buckets of money:* Buying used
can save you a bundle.
*Living under a bridge:* A home
is more than an investment.

## Where's the money?

Chances are you have some money in your checking
account, savings account, wallet and change jar. Gather it
together, count it up and write below.

WHERE'S THE MONEY?   INTEREST RATE?   HOW MUCH?

_____

_____

_____

_____

_____

_____

_____

TOTAL SAVINGS ————————▶

## Moving money for personal gain

Now that it's counted, let's consider moving it around to
make it work for you. You might want to look into an interest-bearing checking account, a savings account or short-
term certificate of deposit. Call your bank and ask about
interest rates for different accounts. The goal is to get your
money to make money. Flip ahead to page 34 if you need
clarification. After you've sorted it out, write below and in
the handy chart on page 48.

WHERE IS IT, NOW?      INTEREST RATE?      HOW MUCH?

_____

_____

_____

_____

_____

_____

_____

TOTAL SAVINGS ————————▶

## Tracking retirement accounts

Do you have a 401(k) plan, Roth IRA, traditional IRA or other retirement account? There are two things you need to know. First, what are these assets worth? And second, are you stuck using them as a retirement account or are they more flexible? Can you use the funds for a down payment on a condo? Can you use the money to pay for graduate school? Find your statement, call the 800 number and ask for the balance. While you have a live duck on the horn, ask if the money in your account can be withdrawn for other purposes. Write your balance below and on page 48 under *retirement*. Don't have a retirement account? Start one. Talk to your bank or consult a financial advisor.

| INVESTMENT | TYPE | AMOUNT |
|---|---|---|
| | | |
| | | |
| | | |
| | | |
| | | |
| | | |
| | | |

TOTAL RETIREMENT ⟶ ▶

## Every month, without fail

By now you have a fairly good idea of your cash value. Every month, around the same day, call your bank or check your statement and track your progress using the chart on page 48. Keep thrifty and you're sure to see some serious upward mobility. Ah, the sweet smell of progress.

---

**Chapter 2 homework: 2-15 minutes**

Order your credit report today! It won't cost you a dime (although you may have to pay if you want to get your credit score). Lots of folks get to see your credit report—credit card companies, mortgage brokers and landlords, to name a few. It's time to get one for yourself. To order, go to www.annualcreditreport.com. When your report arrives, check the info and if you find a mistake, follow the correction instructions. Your report will list all open credit card accounts—you'll need this info in Chapter 4.

☐ Homework complete!

# ◆ THRIFTY TIPS ◆

**Hire a professional**

If I've said it once, I've said it a million times, "Hire a professional!" Hire an accountant, a lawyer or a real estate agent. It will save you time, money and suffering. The right professional, who knows the ins and outs of their business, can save you a ton of cash in no time. Don't think you know everything about everything. Be smart. Know your limitations.

**Net savings**

*Hours of frustration:* You are not going to become an expert in anything in an hour online.

*Embarrassment:* You won't have to hire that professional after you've screwed it up.

Brilliant ideas. Calculations. Notes.

# 3

# WHERE THE HELL?

So, you get your check on Friday, cash it, pay some bills, go out for a cocktail (or three), get a cut plus highlights, brunch with the girls and suddenly it's all gone. Where the hell did it go? You're not living like a princess! Maybe you're spending too much on a two-bedroom filled with plush crap. Maybe you fork over $30 every day on little things that you just don't need. Maybe you just better figure it out!

Once you figure out what the big and little items of life are costing you, the solutions to your financial woes will become very clear. Believe me. Let's say you drop $4 a day at Starbucks. That's a whopping $1,460 a year. Wow! If you quit the joe or make your cup at home, you could spend that green on a week sipping café au lait in Paris or a month at Spanish language camp in Guatemala! It's entirely up to you.

## ◆ THRIFTY TIPS ◆

**Live simple**
You don't need a four-bedroom house. You don't need two cars. You don't need $300 leather boots. Think of our precious planet. Practice downsizing and simplify your life. I used to own a car. When I went thrifty, I gave it up. I don't miss parking tickets, driving around half the night looking for a space, flat tires, broken windows, brushing snow in the winter, road rage, pumping gas, spilling gas, changing tires, drive thru and insurance. I don't even think about that stuff. I raise my right arm and take a cab when a walk is out of the question. In Chicago, it's cheaper.

**Net savings**
*Early departure:* My grandparents have embraced simplicity for 90+ years.
*Shock:* Parking tickets aren't 20 bucks anymore.
*Designated driver status:* I'll take another cosmo, Slim.

## Money in: What do you have to work with?

In this handy chart you're going to figure out how much you made this month—after taxes. If your work is steady, this should be easy to calculate. If you're working three jobs, are self-employed or earn tips, count up your nickels. Did you make any money beyond your regular job? Did you sell your dominatrix outfit (that's so '80s), dog sit for a friend or find $20 on the street? Put a check in the box if it's regular income you can count on every month. Write it all down and count it up. Let's see what you've got to work with.

| JOB/SALE | PAY/MONTH | REGULAR INCOME? |
|----------|-----------|-----------------|
|          |           | ☐ |
|          |           | ☐ |
|          |           | ☐ |
|          |           | ☐ |
|          |           | ☐ |
|          |           | ☐ |
|          |           | ☐ |
|          |           | ☐ |
|          |           | ☐ |
|          |           | ☐ |
|          |           | ☐ |
|          |           | ☐ |
|          |           | ☐ |
|          |           | ☐ |
|          |           | ☐ |
|          |           | ☐ |
|          |           | ☐ |
|          |           | ☐ |
|          |           | ☐ |

TOTAL ──────▶

## Money out: What are your monthly expenses?

Now to answer the question, "Where the hell does it all go?" First, let's look at your monthly expenses—rent or mortgage, your phone(s), utilities, gym membership, movie club—everything. This is all the regular stuff—you get a bill, write a check, affix a stamp—every month. Take a look at this lengthy list. Put a check in the "save?" box if you could spend less or eliminate an expense completely.

| EXPENSE | COST/MONTH | SAVE? |
|---------|-----------|-------|
| | | ☐ |
| | | ☐ |
| | | ☐ |
| | | ☐ |
| | | ☐ |
| | | ☐ |
| | | ☐ |
| | | ☐ |
| | | ☐ |
| | | ☐ |
| | | ☐ |
| | | ☐ |
| | | ☐ |
| | | ☐ |
| | | ☐ |
| | | ☐ |

TOTAL ⟶

## Watch out—little things really add up

The thrifty mandate of the year is, "Watch out for the little things!" You see it, you want it, you buy it! Hey, these things add up—morning coffee $4, *Real Simple* magazine $6, lunch at Siam Noodle $9, tin of Altoids $2, birthday card for Mom $4—that's $25, GONE! On the next page, write down all of your out-of-pocket expenses for four weeks. Don't hesitate!

On the next page, write down all of your out-of-pocket expenses for four weeks.

### ◆ THRIFTY TIPS ◆

**In the thrifty bag**
The answer to many questions is, "It's in the bag." "Do you have any gum?" "You don't have a nail file, do you?" "Got any Kleenex?" "Do you have change for a dollar?"

That's right. It's in the bag—my thrifty bag. I carry it everywhere I go. What else is in the bag? A compact, my cell, a toothbrush, granola bars, some tampons, lip balm, hand cream, a pen, a little notebook, Spanish dictionary, water and my little box o' pills (Advil, Tums and Sudafed). I'm ready for just about anything including a run-in with a young, Spanish-speaking hottie with a migrane.
**Net savings**
*Bleeding gums:* You'll never again clean your teeth with a stick.

# Little things chart

Write today's date in the appropriate square. Note every out-of-pocket expense. Take a look at the example. Start today. No cheating!

| MONDAY | TUESDAY | WEDNESDAY | THURSDAY |
|---|---|---|---|
| 4  *EXAMPLE:*<br>*mocha $3.75*<br>*lunch $7*<br>*fill-up $40*<br>*movie $8*<br>*popcorn $5.25* | | | |
| | | | |
| | | | |
| | | | |

| FRIDAY | SATURDAY | SUNDAY |
|--------|----------|--------|
|        |          |        |
|        |          |        |
|        |          |        |
|        |          |        |

## ◆ THRIFTY TIPS ◆

### Volunteer

Volunteering is a great way to learn a new skill, make new friends, see a play or support a worthy cause. And, it's free. Want to start a new career? Try an internship first. Want to see plays for free? Sign up to usher. Wish you could support your favorite charity? Volunteer your time instead of giving money.

**Net savings**
*Future generations:* The world is a better place, thanks to you.

### Supper club

Want to hang with friends, but too broke to go out? Sounds like the perfect time to start a supper club. Call your friends. Someone brings a couple bottles of wine. Someone bakes lasagna. Someone makes a salad and picks up a loaf of bread. Don't forget dessert. Switch around so you don't always get stuck cooking. Serves 6-8.

**Net savings**
*Bloated tab:* Drinks are a hell of a lot cheaper served at home.

# ◆ THRIFTY TIPS ◆

**Shop in your own closet**
Have you ever bought a new pair of shoes only to discover another pair JUST LIKE IT in your closet? Well, at least your taste hasn't changed. Next time you get the urge to splurge, go shopping in your closet. I think you'll be pleasantly surprised. Last time I looked, I found this cashmere sweater. It's perfect for December in Chicago, it's free and I didn't even have to leave the house! Who knew?
**Net savings**
*Shopping hours:* You don't even have to get dressed to go on a spree.
*Storage space:* Who has room for identical pairs of shoes?

**Used treasure**
You've heard that expression, "One girl's trash is another girl's treasure?" Buying stuff used can save tons of money—try garage sales, classifieds, www.ebay.com and thrift stores.
**Net savings**
*Wearing:* With no effort on your part, your jeans have that "well-worn" look.

## The numbers speak for themselves
Daily stuff adds up fast. Crunch the numbers. What are you spending every month on lunch? Coffee? Clothes? Manicures? Gifts? Movies? Do you spend more on the little things than your rent or mortgage? I'm sure you'll be inspired to change some of your expensive habits and use the money to bankroll more important short-term and long-term goals. Are you all fired up? Look at the chart on page 54, then crunch!

_____

_____

_____

_____

_____

## You don't have to give it up
You don't always have to quit something to save money. Let's say every day around 3 pm you get a little craving for something chocolate—you know that craving—so you pop down to the vending machine in the basement and fork over $1 or more for some peanut M&Ms. What's that costing you? $5/wk X 52= about $250 a year. On M&Ms? Wow! You could buy your chocolate in bulk and save a bundle. Pick it up at the grocery store, Costco, wherever. What did you give up? NOTHING. What can you save, about $150 a year. Bonus. Why not make a list of the things you don't want to give up but could save money on.

| DON'T GIVE UP | AMOUNT SAVED/1 YR |
|---|---|
| | |
| | |
| | |
| | |
| TOTAL SAVED ⟶ | |

## Your very own *quit list*

Have any bad habits that burn green? You know the ones I'm talking about—the things that make you fat, irritable and unattractive. These habits might even be killing you—smoking, boozing, eating junk and driving everywhere. The solution? QUIT. Quit smoking. Quit boozing. Quit junk and start walking. I'll help you start! Here's an empty quit list. Go ahead and fill it in! Look at how much you're going to save!

QUIT _____ AMOUNT SAVED/1 YR

_____

_____

_____

_____

_____

_____

_____

TOTAL SAVED ——————▶

## Just cut back

So, you don't want to quit. Fine, be that way. How about cutting back? Maybe you eat out three times a week. How about cutting back to just two? Why not make another list? Calculate what you'd save.

CUT BACK _____ AMOUNT SAVED/1 YR

_____

_____

_____

_____

_____

TOTAL SAVED ——————▶

## ◆ THRIFTY TIPS ◆

**Super quick dinners**
Life is exhausting. Going out and ordering in is expensive. Stock up on frozen and practically instant dinners. It will keep you sane and make you rich.
**Net savings**
*Wishful thinking:* The delivery guy is not your future husband.

**Living with the 'rents**
Living can be expensive. If you need to drastically reduce your spending, consider moving back in with your parents for a spell. I know it sounds drastic, but everyone seems to be doing it. Think of how much money you could save! I recommend that you decide in advance how long this experiment will last. Give yourself a deadline—six months or a year. Make sure you're really saving money. You don't want to get stuck there forever.
**Net savings**
*WOW, buckets:* Rent, food, utilities and more.
*Hours on the phone with Mom and Dad:* You live with them, you can just yell down the hall.

## ◆ THRIFTY TIPS ◆

### Get covered

Don't have renter's insurance? What are you waiting for—a fire, a flood? I can hear it now, "Renter's insurance? I can barely afford the rent!" You like rolling the dice every day? You think it won't happen to you: "I don't smoke after sex. I won't burn the place to the ground." Hmm. Thinking like this always gets you screwed.

Think your landlord's insurance covers your stuff? No way. Your landlord probably has insurance, but it covers the building, not your flat screen TV, not your favorite Kenneth Cole boots, not your Cuisinart or CD collection. Nothing. Look around your place and get some insurance today!

### Net Savings

*Pain and suffering:* If disaster hits, grab your bag and go shopping!

## Progress report

☐ Have you quit bitching?
☐ Have you balanced your checkbook lately?
☐ Have you started your emergency fund?
☐ Have you made short-term goals?
☐ Have you made long-term goals?
☐ Did you order your credit report?
☐ Are you keeping track all of the little things?
☐ Are you stocking up on non-perishables?
☐ Are you changing expensive habits?
☐ Can you lower any monthly expenses?
☐ Are you tracking your retirement accounts?
☐ Are you quitting bad habits?
☐ Do you have renter's insurance?
☐ Are you making thrifty progress?

You're doing great! Keep going, girl!

---

### Chapter 3 homework: 2-11 minutes

What does your car cost every month?
Add it up!

| | |
|---|---|
| monthly car payment | $_____ |
| insurance | _____ |
| gas | _____ |
| maintenance | _____ |
| parking | _____ |
| tickets | _____ |
| other | _____ |
| TOTAL | |

Ouch. If you're an urban girl, that's miles of public transport or a lot of cab rides!

☐ Homework complete!

# HAS YOUR CREDIT REPORT ARRIVED?

Have you been ignoring your homework? I promise it won't hurt. If you've been delinquent about ordering your report, do it today. You can order it online. Simply visit www.annualcreditreport.com. The report should be free. However, you may have to pay to get your credit score or FICO score. I'm not going to discuss credit scores; entire books have been devoted to the topic. If you want to know your score, go ahead and request it. Otherwise, just order your report. You may be able to get it immediately or you may have to wait for it to arrive via the mail. It doesn't matter—just do it!

When your report arrives, read it! Check it over to make sure there are no mistakes. Check all the information. If you find a mistake, follow the instructions included with the report and take care of it right away. Don't delay.

**Why is your credit report important?**
Chances are high that someday you will need to buy something on credit—a house or a car. You will need excellent credit to get the best (lowest) interest rate. If your credit is mediocre, you may pay a much higher rate. And if your credit is dismal, you may not be able to get a loan at all.

**Here are ways to keep your credit in good shape:**
1. Pay ALL your bills on time (credit cards, rent, mortgage, phone, cable, everything).
2. Don't go over the limit on your credit cards.
3. Don't max out your credit cards.
4. Don't apply for a new credit card if you don't need to.
5. Pay more than the minimum balance on your credit cards every cycle (even if it's only $5 more—this should improve your credit score).
6. Minimize or eliminate your credit card balance(s).
7. Don't overburden yourself with debt, credit card, car, mortgage, etc.
8. Pay off debt rather than just moving it around.
9. If you are having problems paying bills, call your creditors, explain the situation and try to make a deal.
10. Check your credit report regularly to be sure the information is accurate. This can be your first defense against identity theft.

# ◆ THRIFTY TIPS ◆

### Your precious wheels
Everyone says you can't live without a car. Would I get your attention if I said you could retire 10 years earlier if you got rid of your precious wheels? Public transportation has never been better!

### Net savings
*Stress:* Say goodbye to road rage.
*Felony conviction:* You never feel the urge to hit someone when you're walking.
*Annoyance:* You never have to talk to a car insurance company again.
*A wad:* I'd say thousands.

### Pamper thy self
Are you stressed out? Do you need a break from reality? A little ME time? Don't drop $200 at a downtown spa. Take a hot bubble bath, enjoy a glass of chardonnay on the porch or cuddle up with a good book. Don't have time? MAKE TIME. Open your calendar right now and find an open evening.

### Net savings
*Sanity:* You don't feel like throwing yourself out the window anymore.

Brilliant ideas. Calculations. Notes.

# 4

# DIG YOURSELF OUT!

Don't panic over your plastic. Get out your calculator and learn how to multiply again. You'll figure out exactly how much you owe and what it costs you every month. You won't believe what you're paying in interest. Together, we'll make a strategy for getting out of debt quickly and legally.

This could be the most painful chapter of your life. My guess is you have no idea how much credit card debt you have. Am I right? If you're in the black (don't have any debt), you are my superhero! Congratulations, you have passed a grueling test. Your reward: Skip this chapter!

**The artist inside**

So, you're an artist inside — stuck in a boring, going-nowhere-fast job. Congratulations. Let me go get a shiny medal and pin it on your creative butt. Stop whining. You have two options. One — put together an outstanding portfolio, go get a creative job and quit kvetching. Or two — funnel your creative energy into a hobby — make a bracelet, knit a scarf, build a sand castle, whatever. Try to figure out what you really need to fill the creative void. Don't kid yourself. Having a creative job can be plenty of headache and everyone's a critic. I know.

**Net savings**

*Abandonment:* Your friends will return after you stop all the complaining.

## How much do you owe?

Have debt? Don't panic. We will get to the bottom of it together. You'll need to dig through that pile of papers on your desk and pull out your credit card statements. Then, you'll fill in the next chart. You may need to call each credit company to get current info. If you're feeling stressed, pour yourself a glass of vino. Ready? Let's just start by listing all the cards you have including the ones with a $0 balance, along with some card info. Take a look at your trusty credit report. It will list all open accounts.

| CARD NAME | PHONE NUMBER | BALANCE |
|-----------|--------------|---------|
| | | |
| | | |
| | | |
| | | |
| | | |
| | | |
| | | |
| | | |
| | | |
| | | |
| | | |
| | | |
| | | |
| | | |
| | | |
| | | |
| | | |
| | | |
| | | |
| | | |

TOTAL CREDIT CARD BALANCE ⟶

## What's this debt costing you, darling?

I'm not trying to depress you or inspire an anxiety attack. These are just numbers you should know. Get your calculator. In the next chart, you will multiply the amount of your debt by the interest rate. This will give you the approximate amount of interest you pay a year.

You might need to get yourself another glass of "juice." Don't panic about the math. I'll give you a quick lesson.

Math lesson: 19% is equal to .19 and 9% is equal to .09. So, if you have $5,000 of debt at 19%, the math looks like this: $5000 x .19 = $950. $950 is the approximate amount of interest you are paying per year. If you want to know how much per month, you divide $950 by 12. The math looks like this: $950 ÷ 12 = $79.16666666 or about $79 in interest a month.

| CARD NAME | % | BALANCE | COST/YR | COST/MO |
|---|---|---|---|---|
|  |  |  |  |  |
|  |  |  |  |  |
|  |  |  |  |  |
|  |  |  |  |  |
|  |  |  |  |  |
|  |  |  |  |  |
|  |  |  |  |  |
|  |  |  |  |  |
|  |  |  |  |  |
|  |  |  |  |  |
|  |  |  |  |  |
|  |  |  |  |  |
| TOTAL |  |  |  |  |

## For the record

*Thrifty Girl* is NOT a magician. If you have lots of credit card debt, you should consider talking to a professional—a financial counselor or a bankruptcy attorney. What is a lot of debt? If your debt equals more than six months of your income or if you feel you will never be able to pay it off.

**Tracking your career**

Do you know what you want to be when you grow up? Relax, I didn't either. I tried reading *What Color is Your Parachute?* I'd rather put a fork in my eye. If you don't have a clue where your career will take you, try to find a direction. That's right DIRECTION. It will be much easer if you start on a path that leads from one career to another. For example, I started with a degree in set design, worked in theater and film, landed a job in special events décor, hated it, quit to take a few classes in graphic design, started teaching graphics classes and now work as a graphic artist. I did a whole bunch of things, but didn't veer far from the visual artist path. I didn't need to get another degree, just another portfolio.

**Net savings**

*Wall space:* For most of us, one diploma is enough.

## Transfer balances to save your soul

As far as credit card debt goes, there are two important factors—the balance and the interest rate. Don't underestimate the importance of the rate. Think about it—$10,000 of debt at 19% costs about $1,900 a year; at 3% it's only around $300. That's a huge difference, $1,600 to be exact! So, how are you going to get that 3%? In a word: TRANSFER for a teaser rate. Credit card companies use short-term teaser rates to entice you to transfer a balance to their card. These rates usually last only six months, then the rate jumps up much higher.

## Call your cards and get some info

So, call ALL your cards (including all of the ones with a $0 balance), ask the following questions and fill in the chart on the next page.

1. How much can I transfer to this card?
   (Write the answer in TRANSFER ALLOWED.)
2. Is there a fee for the transfer? Would you be willing to waive the fee if I transfer more than, say, $10,000 (or whatever you think you will be transfering)?
   (Write the answer in FEE.)
3. What is the interest rate on the transfer?
   (Write the answer in TEASER %.)
4. How long does this rate last?
   (Write the answer in RATE TERM.)
5. What will the rate jump to after the teaser rate ends?
   (Write the answer in JUMP %.)
6. I'm going to transfer my balance to another card. Would you lower my current rate if I kept my balance with you?

   Hell, it's worth a try! If they will change your rate, you might not have to transfer. Make sure to ask how long the new rate will last.

| CARD NAME | TRANSFER ALLOWED | FEE | TEASER % | RATE TERM | JUMP % |
|-----------|------------------|-----|----------|-----------|--------|
|           |                  |     |          |           |        |
|           |                  |     |          |           |        |
|           |                  |     |          |           |        |
|           |                  |     |          |           |        |
|           |                  |     |          |           |        |
|           |                  |     |          |           |        |
|           |                  |     |          |           |        |
|           |                  |     |          |           |        |
|           |                  |     |          |           |        |
|           |                  |     |          |           |        |
|           |                  |     |          |           |        |
|           |                  |     |          |           |        |
|           |                  |     |          |           |        |
|           |                  |     |          |           |        |
|           |                  |     |          |           |        |
|           |                  |     |          |           |        |
|           |                  |     |          |           |        |
|           |                  |     |          |           |        |
| TOTAL     |                  |     |          |           |        |

## Why is the total transfer allowed such a big deal?

It tells you how flexible you are (this is starting to sound like a yoga class). The more money you can transfer, the easier it is to reduce your interest rate. A lower interest rate means slower debt growth. And that means you can get out of debt faster and cheaper.

## What's the deal with fees?

Some credit card companies charge a fee to transfer. It's not a bad idea to ask if they will waive the fee. It's worth a try. There is no reason to avoid a transfer just because there's a fee. However, it's always good to know what things cost. For most large transfers, paying a $35 fee is worth it. In the example on the previous page, you're going to save $1,600 a year, so a $35 transfer fee is chicken scratch.

## Manage your credit cards – prepare to transfer

Now look at the "What's it costing?" chart on page 23 and reorder your cards based on the interest rate. Write the card with the highest interest rate first, the next highest second and so on.

| CARD NAME | BALANCE | % RATE | EXPIRES | JUMP % | TRANSFER ALLOWED |
|-----------|---------|--------|---------|--------|------------------|
|           |         |        |         |        |                  |
|           |         |        |         |        |                  |
|           |         |        |         |        |                  |
|           |         |        |         |        |                  |
|           |         |        |         |        |                  |
|           |         |        |         |        |                  |
|           |         |        |         |        |                  |
|           |         |        |         |        |                  |
|           |         |        |         |        |                  |
|           |         |        |         |        |                  |
|           |         |        |         |        |                  |
|           |         |        |         |        |                  |
|           |         |        |         |        |                  |
|           |         |        |         |        |                  |
|           |         |        |         |        |                  |
|           |         |        |         |        |                  |
|           |         |        |         |        |                  |
|           |         |        |         |        |                  |
|           |         |        |         |        |                  |
|           |         |        |         |        |                  |
|           |         |        |         |        |                  |
|           |         |        |         |        |                  |
|           |         |        |         |        |                  |
|           |         |        |         |        |                  |
|           |         |        |         |        |                  |

## Transfer

What's the plan? You want to transfer balances with high interest rates to cards with low teaser rates. It's best if you can completely pay off a card (get it down to a $0 balance). Then you can transfer another high interest rate balance to the card with a $0 balance for another teaser rate. So, keep a balance on a card as long as you get a teaser rate. Before the teaser rate expires, transfer again. When you pay off a card, cross it off and write it in again at the bottom of the list with a $0 balance. Continue to use the chart on the previous page. For clarification, look at the sample below.

## SAMPLE

Start by writing in your card information like this:

| CARD NAME | BALANCE | % RATE | EXPIRES | JUMP % | TRANSFER ALLOWED |
|-----------|---------|--------|---------|--------|------------------|
| Capital | $10,000 | .18 | NA | NA | $0 |
| Global | $2,000 | .16 | NA | NA | $5,000 |
| Express | $0 | .03 | 6/09 | .16 | $11,000 |

Call Express and transfer $10,000 from Capital to Express. Then strike out both cards in your chart. Your chart will look like this:

| CARD NAME | BALANCE | % RATE | EXPIRES | JUMP % | TRANSFER ALLOWED |
|-----------|---------|--------|---------|--------|------------------|
| ~~Capital~~ | ~~$10,000~~ | ~~.18~~ | ~~NA~~ | ~~NA~~ | ~~$0~~ |
| Global | $2,000 | .16 | NA | NA | $5,000 |
| ~~Express~~ | ~~$0~~ | ~~.03~~ | ~~6/09~~ | ~~.16~~ | ~~$11,000~~ |

Write in the new balances on the Capital card ($0) and the Express card ($10,000). Complete Capital and Express row with any new information. Your chart will look like this:

| CARD NAME | BALANCE | % RATE | EXPIRES | JUMP % | TRANSFER ALLOWED |
|-----------|---------|--------|---------|--------|------------------|
| ~~Capital~~ | ~~$10,000~~ | ~~.18~~ | ~~NA~~ | ~~NA~~ | ~~$0~~ |
| Global | $2,000 | .16 | NA | NA | $5,000 |
| ~~Express~~ | ~~$0~~ | ~~.03~~ | ~~6/09~~ | ~~.16~~ | ~~$11,000~~ |
| Capital | $0 | .02 | 12/09 | .18 | $10,000 |
| Express | $10,000 | .03 | 6/09 | .16 | $1,000 |

The total balance hasn't changed—it's still $12,000. But, the interest on $10,000 was reduced drastically, from 18% ($150 a month) to 3% ($25 a month). You saved $125 a month from one transfer! Now, the Capital card has a $0 balance. Tomorrow, call Capital and ask to transfer $2,000 from Global to Capital for another teaser rate. Repeat and save!

**Makin' copies**

No, I'm not talking about photocopies of your "best side." I mean copies of important documents and keys. This can save you bundles in the wasted time and aggravation department. Make duplicates of your birth certificate, driver's license, passport, lease, car title, etc. Store them in a safe place outside of your home—locked up at work or in a safety deposit box. Make copies of all-important keys and keep them in a convenient spot. You'll thank me later.

**Net savings**

*Insanity:* Stop running around like a nut in your PJs, late for an interview, locked out of the house.

**Paying for cash**

I'd say ATM fees are out of control. I was charged $3.50 to get cash in Las Vegas recently, good grief! Do yourself a favor, save a few bucks a week by avoiding these fees. Get cash for free from your bank's ATM. (They shouldn't charge if you have an account.)

**Net savings**

*Ouch:* 2-4% on every hit!

## 14 Ways to beat the cards

1. Don't pay late. Pay early or pay on time, but NEVER, EVER pay late.
2. Never go over your limit.
3. Always pay more than the minimum payment (even if it's just $5, it should help your credit score).
4. Avoid cash advances like the plague.
5. Put all new charges on a card with no balance and pay the new balance in full every month. That's right: I said, IN FULL EVERY MONTH.
6. Transfer balances to minimize interest payments.
7. Try to pay your bill when it ARRIVES. Don't wait 'til it's due.
8. If you screw up (late payment, over your limit, etc.), call your company and cry, beg and promise never to do it again. Try to get them to remove the penalty charges.
9. Skip the credit; pay cash.
10. Don't apply for any new cards.
11. Don't cancel any cards until you're out of debt. You need them to boost your transfer flexibility.
12. Mark the date each payment needs to be SENT on a calendar.
13. Use the money you're saving by transfering to pay down your balances.
14. Try not to max out your cards.

## Maxed out?

If your cards are all filled up and you can't transfer, it's time for plan B. If you have a small amount of debt you think you will be able to pay off, you might consider opening a new credit card account with a low teaser rate and transfer one or more of your old balances to it. If you have lots of debt and think you may never be able to dig yourself out, it's time to talk to a financial counselor or bankruptcy attorney. Don't stress. You are not the first, nor will you be the last, girl to consider bankruptcy.

Brilliant ideas. Calculations. Notes.

## ◆ THRIFTY TIPS ◆

**Thrifty diet**

You'll just die it's so simple. Eat less, cut out sugary crap, don't eat after 7pm, drink water and walk 20+ minutes every day. Finally, you'll be able to squeeze into every-thing in your closet. And think of all the money you'll save!

**Net savings**

*Tons:* You look great without eating that nasty diet food.

**Auto everything**

Just about all my bill pay-ments are deducted auto-matically from my checking account. I love it! I don't need to write a check, lick an enve-lope or find a stamp. It saves time, money and resources. Sometimes it even reduces your interest rate (about .5% on my student loans). How-ever, make sure to note the auto payment in your check-book! Don't forget. You don't want to be overdrawn!

**Net savings**

*Sickness and death:* Remember the *Seinfeld* episode when George's fiancée dies? It could happen!

---

## Chapter 4 homework: 2-21 minutes

Pay off one card and use it for purchases. You shouldn't be buying stuff on cards with a balance. Why? You're probably paying interest on new purchases in addition to the interest on your balance. So, your best bet is to pay off one card (get it down to a $0 balance) and use it for shopping. As long as you pay your balance IN FULL, ON TIME every month, most cards won't charge any interest on new purchases. It's like getting a free 30-day loan. And, don't be an idiot: Leave the rest of your cards at home.

☐ Homework complete!

# 5 TIME IS YOUR SLAVE

You want to get out of debt. Great, but you also want to start saving for retirement and start an emergency fund. Oh, and you really want to go to your best friend's wedding in Las Vegas in six months. "How," you ask, "can I do it all?"

You obviously can't just crawl into a hole while you get out of debt or save for retirement. *Thrifty Girl* doesn't want you to suffer. Who wants to spend the whole winter eating pasta from a can? That's not living. If you want to go to that Vegas wedding, you'll have to start planning.

You're smart and you're a multitasker. Your money needs to multitask, too. Plan ahead. Be diligent. Put some green toward your credit card debt, a couple of bucks in your retirement fund, a bit in the emergency fund and set some aside for the wedding. This way, your debt is ALWAYS shrinking and your savings are ALWAYS growing.

Start being proactive. In addition to balancing multiple goals, get in the habit of saving for things. That's right, SAVING. And my personal advice on Vegas? Thanks for the free drinks; skip the blackjack table.

## Four short-term goals that could change your life

Remember way back in Chapter 1 when I said, "Quit bitching!" Well, I've been going on for pages. Now it's your turn. You need to come up with four inexpensive (under $300), short-term (under one year) goals. These goals could be going to a friend's wedding (you need to buy a dress and a gift), or maybe your cell phone is acting grumpy and you need to get a new one. You're actually going to write these goals down—along with the cost—in the order of importance. The most important should go on the top of the list and we'll work our way down. Feel free to check back on your original short-term goals on page 4 for inspiration and direction.

Now the difficult part. You're not going to just run out and charge up a storm—oh no. You are going to save for these objects of desire. That's right. You can use a piggy bank, a jar or a savings account. When you accumulate the right amount, you can spend it, not a moment sooner. Write your four goals below and your first priority on page 48 in the *savings* chart.

| GOAL | PRICE TAG |
|------|-----------|
| 1 | |
| 2 | |
| 3 | |
| 4 | |

◆ THRIFTY TIPS ◆

**Cash allowance**
Putting it on plastic seems so easy until you get the bill and burst an artery looking at the bottom line. If you're a plastic junkie, leave your cards at home and start paying cash. Give yourself a weekly cash allowance for all out-of-pocket expenses. When it's gone, it's gone. I think you'll figure it out really fast!
**Net savings**
*Trip to the hospital:* You won't bat an eye at your balance.

**Fill 'er up**
From what I've read, Friday is the busiest and most expensive day at the pumps. So, it seems wise to fill your tank at the beginning of the week—let's say Monday through Wednesday when you can beat the crowds and save a few nickels.
**Net savings**
*Noxious fumes:* Waiting in line for the pump with the motor running is killing you slowly.

## ◆ THRIFTY TIPS ◆

**Staying or moving**
Let's face it—moving is hell. No one loves moving. Moving is expensive. By the time you look for a new place, pack up all your crap, rent a truck or hire movers, take a day off of work and lose part of your security deposit, you've spent a grand if you've spent a dime. If you're moving for financial reasons, do the math before you start collecting empty boxes from the liquor store.

**Net savings**
*Chiropractor bills:* I hear flat screens are really light, but your old TV weighs a ton. Oh, my back!

**How you spend it**
You are going to make a finite amount of money in your life. It is how you spend it that will determine whether your life is a constant struggle or a comfortable journey. Don't wait to get a raise, win the Lotto or inherit from Uncle George. Spend wisely. Start today.

**Net savings**
*Regret:* No amount of top-shelf vodka will make it go away.

## Four long-term goals to banish regret

Life is short. The older you get, the faster time flies. It's high time to start thinking about long-term goals. You probably have a fairly good idea of at least a couple life-long goals. Maybe you want to buy a place or go back to school. Once again, you're going to have to save. If you're going to buy a place, you'll need to save for a down payment (usually 5-20%). If you're going back to school, you should ask yourself how much money it will cost—tuition, books, living expenses, etc. Things always seem more expensive when you need to save up front. In order of importance, list your goals and what they will cost. We're going to tackle these one at a time! Store your money in a savings account or CD (certificate of deposit) where it can grow. Write four goals below and your first priority on page 48 under *savings*.

| GOAL | PRICE TAG |
|------|-----------|
| 1 | |
| 2 | |
| 3 | |
| 4 | |

## Progress report time

☐ Have you balanced your checkbook lately?
☐ How's that emergency fund going?
☐ Did you order your credit report?
☐ Are you keeping track of all the little things?
☐ Are you transferring credit card debt to teaser rates?
☐ Are you paying your credit card bill early?
☐ Did you pay off one credit card for new purchases?

Check off your accomplishments and give yourself a big hug. You go!

Brilliant ideas. Calculations. Notes.

## ◆ THRIFTY TIPS ◆

**Eat out, spend less**
Order one glass of wine and stick to the entrée. What? You need more food than a restaurant entrée? Says who? Forget about appetizers, salad, dessert and coffee — the entrée is the biggest bang for your buck in any restaurant.
**Net savings**
*Pounds:* You know the deal — eat it now; wear it later.

**Thrifty "better" half**
There is nothing more wasteful than mastering thrift only to hook-up with someone who spends money like a bachelor at a strip club. Let's be honest, couples fight over money, withhold sex over money and even get divorced over money. It's best if you and your other have an "understanding," as they say, about finances. If you can't find someone thrifty, I have words for you: separate checking, separate credit cards and mandatory "pre-nup."
**Net savings**
*Alimony:* You think it's only guys who pay? You pay.

**Chapter 5 homework: 2-15 minutes**
You will need:
1 jar or other small container
1 photo of your #1 short-term goal
  (cut from a magazine or catalog)
some tape

Tape the photo to the jar. Search the bottom of your purse, check your pockets and reach behind the couch. If you find any coins, put them in the jar. Every day, drop your spare change into the jar. Watch it accumulate. If you skip your $4 morning coffee, make a special contribution to the jar. It's like paying yourself!

☐ Homework complete!

# A COUPLE OF SAVINGS OPTIONS

## Checking

These days, everyone needs a checking account. If you don't have one, go get one. What? Are you going to pay your rent in cash? Balance your account regularly. Don't forget to log direct deposits, ATM withdrawals, auto payments and transfers as well as checks. However, if you want your money to make money, a checking account is no place to let it stay. Keep what you will need for the month and transfer the rest to an interest-bearing account. Your money is FDIC insured (usually to $100,000) and can't lose value.

## Interest-bearing checking

As the name suggests, this is a checking account that will pay you interest on your balance. Unfortunately, these accounts usually require a higher minimum balance and offer a low, fluctuating interest rate. Your money is FDIC insured (usually to $100,000) and can't lose value.

## Savings

Savings accounts are fine for storing your hard-earned dough for short stints. You can usually open an account with as little as $100. The interest rates are fairly minimal and often change, but you can withdraw your money at any time. It's not a bad place to start your emergency savings fund. Your money is FDIC insured (usually to $100,000) and can't lose value.

## Certificate of deposit (CD)

CDs are a great place to store cash. Your money will be earning a higher interest rate than an interest-bearing checking account or a savings account. The rate is locked in for the duration of the CD (1 month, 3 months, 6 months, etc.). So, when you open the account, you will know exactly how much interest you will receive. However, there is usually a penalty for early withdrawal of your investment, and CDs frequently require a higher minimum balance than a savings account. If you think you'll need the dough next week, don't open a 3-month CD. Your money is FDIC insured (usually to $100,000) and can't lose value.

## Other investments

There are a slew of other investment options out there—stocks, bonds, mutual funds, etc. Be careful. Many investment options can lose value. Please don't come crying to me when you lose your skirt in the market.

# STEER CLEAR OF DISASTER

That's right, it's time to get organized and learn how to steer clear of total disaster. I'm sure this seems like a huge undertaking and you're thinking, "This is it. I've had enough. It's time to ditch this preachy book, hail a cab and go out for an expensive sushi dinner—with sake."

Stay calm (deep-blue-ocean, deep-blue-ocean). You're making great progress. Just think of all your thrifty accomplishments. Don't underestimate your achievements. You're in the home stretch; just a few more details to attend to. I promise there will be time for snack breaks.

**Annual purge**
Spring cleaning is so 1958. I do autumn purge. Here's how it works: Every year, around September, go though the house and get rid of anything that's just taking up space. Try it. If you have anything valuable, sell it. You can list it on www.ebay.com or put up a sign in the laundry room. Donate the crap that's worthless to you to Goodwill. If you itemize your deductions, save your donation receipt.
**Net savings**
*Storage space:* Plenty of room now that the crap is gone.
*Taxes:* Aren't you hot shit? You have deductions.

# FIRST, GET ORGANIZED
## Big box of receipts

Usually I recommend getting rid of stuff. Now, I'm actually going to propose saving something: receipts. I have a box about the size of a shoebox. I save every receipt—grocery receipts, clothing receipts, lunch receipts—everything. Why? First, you need your receipt to return anything these days. If you have something you never used or stuff that broke when you looked at it, get the receipt and RETURN IT! Second, you need receipts if you qualify for tax deductions. Ask your new best friend—your accountant. This all sounds great! Get yourself a box and start saving now! Go ahead. Chop-chop.

## A calendar should do the trick

To stay organized, you will need a calendar. You don't need to buy one. Find something free or print one off the internet. Put it in a place you can't miss. I have mine stuck to the fridge. Got stuff you don't want to forget? Put it on the calendar. Start with financial stuff—the day your credit card bill, electric bill and rent or mortgage need to be SENT. This is different from the day it's due, right? When you get sick of buying stamps, you can embrace autowithdrawl and skip the calendar. Finally, mark down the personal stuff you need to remember—birthdays, anniversaries, doctor's appointments, etc.

The trick is to actually LOOK at the calendar regularly. Don't just look at today. Look ahead to see what's coming down the pike. Oh, Mom's birthday is at the end of the month. It's time to start thinking about a gift so you won't have to fork over the big bucks to FedEx at the last minute.

## A place for almost everything

If you're the sort who can never find anything in your place—a pair of scissors, the wine bottle opener, a pen with ink, the phone book—it's time to get organized. Try making a place for categories of crap. I have a box for wrapping paper, decorative bags, ribbon and gift boxes. I have a dresser drawer with office supplies. I even keep all my black T-shirts together. It makes it a hell of a lot easier to find everything. Who wants to feel like life is an ongoing archeological dig?

How does this save money? Let's say you go shopping for something you really need—like 100W lightbulbs. The next day, you open a drawer or closet to discover, you guessed it, boxes of 100W lightbulbs. Where the hell were those yesterday? I had no idea I had bulbs in the house.

Staying organized and keeping stuff in a particular spot saves plenty of green and shopping energy.

## Make a list

If there ever was a list girl, I'm it. I've really perfected this list thing. I have a list for stuff I need to do at work, another for stuff to do at home, a reading list, a movie list, a list of million dollar ideas and a grocery list. Thank God I don't actually have a list of lists. It's your typical Post-it note party—yellow everywhere.

## NOW, STEER CLEAR OF TOTAL DISASTER
### Accountants all 'round

If you complain about accountants and lawyers, please stop. Most times they are worth their weight in gold. The first time I used an accountant for my taxes, I figure she saved me $3,000. Don't think that $150 an hour is highway robbery when a good accountant can save you thousands in a single hour. Find a good accountant before tax time!

## Insurance for YOUR lifestyle

The right insurance can save your little tail any day of the week. Don't cut corners on health insurance, car insurance or renter's insurance. Life insurance is only for girls with dependents—a spouse, child or even a parent.

| YOU HAVE | YOU NEED | YOU SHOULD GET |
|---|---|---|
| ☐ Health | ☐ Health | ☐ Health |
| ☐ Renter's | ☐ Renter's | ☐ Renter's |
| ☐ Car | ☐ Car | ☐ Car |
| ☐ Life | ☐ Life | ☐ Life |

## A living will

Two things are for sure—you are alive now and you will die some day. You need two wills. Let's talk about living first. I'm sure you trust your spouse or family to make the right decision if you ever have the bad luck to land in a coma after a car accident. However, I'd rather be safe than sorry. I surely don't want to sit around rotting in a hospital bed after my brain has turned to mush. When my brain is gone, I'm out o' here! A living will allows YOU to determine when you would like to stay plugged in and when you would like to go. It's a dandy idea to have one.

## A dying will

I know it's kind of nasty to talk about dying, but it's better to get it out of the way while you're young and you think death is a long way off. Everyone should have a will. It won't make life sweeter for you—you'll be dead. However, it will make things much easier for friends and family when you experience the inevitable. It's a real pain in the ass when folks die without a will.

Brilliant ideas. Calculations. Notes.

**Chapter 6 homework: 12-30 minutes**

Work on getting the right insurance. You can usually save a bit of green if you purchase multiple insurance policies (like renter's insurance and car insurance) from one provider.

☐ Homework complete!

## ◆ THRIFTY TIPS ◆

**The value of friends**
If it weren't for my friends, I wouldn't have lived to write this itty-bitty book. If you have great friends, cherish them. If your friends suck, get new ones.
**Net savings**
*Time on the couch:* Friends are better than counseling and drugs most days.

**The dreaded second job**
Every now and then I hear some financial guru recommending that you can cure your financial blues by getting a second job. My guess is these folks have never had a second job. Are you tired after working all week? Imagine how drained you would feel if you had a second job. Before you decide to run out and get a bartending job, crunch the numbers. How much will you make? How much will it cost you? Will you have added transportation, food or clothing expenses? Is it really worth it?
**Net savings**
*Exhaustion:* Aren't you too old to be working 20 hours a day?

# 7

# KICK EVERY STONE

Here are some tips and tricks. Do you think you can learn the tips and tricks and ditch the rest of the book? Please, as they say, "Stick to the program!" Here are some big ones to keep you on track:

☐ Avoid driving everywhere
☐ Give up expensive bad habits
☐ Skip dining out; start a supper club
☐ Dump your land line
☐ Get the right insurance
☐ Carry a thrifty bag
☐ Drink water instead of carbonated crap
☐ Get plenty of rest
☐ Eat less food and drink less booze
☐ Leave your credit cards at home
☐ Bring lunch to work
☐ Get organized, stay organized
☐ Entertain at home

☐ Buy a modest place to live
☐ Avoid credit card and bank fees
☐ Travel off-peak
☐ Buy used
☐ Quit saving crap you don't need
☐ Watch out for the little things
☐ Balance your checkbook regularly
☐ Forget about the past; focus on the future
☐ Find a job that you enjoy
☐ Spend less than you make
☐ Plan ahead
☐ Stock up
☐ Take care of yourself and your stuff

Check off the ones you have already done. Damn you're good! Keep going!

## Cheap, fast and easy

Having fun doesn't have to break the bank. Think of all the cheap, fast and easy enjoyment that's out there! For example, walking, running, hiking, biking, hot shower, hot bath, gardening, relaxing, daydreaming, swimming, baking, hanging out (remember when we just used to hang out?), conversations, letters, emails, the library, architectural appreciation, parks, team sports, museums, cafes, people watching, playing music, listening to music, learning to juggle, board games, cooking, jump rope, playing cards, having a swearing contest, ice cream, movie rental, reading, napping, art galleries. My favorites? Ice cream and a hot bath. I've given you a bunch of ideas. Now, you make your own list!

_____
_____
_____
_____
_____
_____
_____
_____
_____
_____
_____

### ◆ THRIFTY TIPS ◆

**Semi-retirement**
I dream about semi-retirement. My heaven is working 20 flexible hours a week and making $30,000 a year. Doesn't that sound freeing? I could spend the whole winter in Mexico! I don't want to work my ass off until I'm 65 and then dive head first into the abyss of retirement. I'd rather work part-time FOREVER.

**Net savings**
_The tedium of a retirement party:_ You'll never need one.

Is there anything more expensive than going to a wedding? God, the last one must have set me back a grand—and I wasn't even IN the wedding. It's usually no big deal if the wedding is in your neighborhood. But if you have to travel, stay in a hotel, rent a car, buy a dress and find a gift ... ouch, it all adds up! My advice? Unless it's someone very close—your best-best friend, your sibling or a parent— don't go. Send a card.

**Net savings**
*Big money:* Let's face it. If it were free, you would love to go.
*Running around like a nut all summer:* Open a bottle of pino and admire your reflection in the pool.

## Your personal *It Can Wait* list

I'm sure you've had your impulsive moments. You see something you want and you just whip out the plastic and buy it on the spot. Try to avoid see-want-buy syndrome. Curb the impulse by making an *It Can Wait* list. Write the date, the item and the approximate price. If you just wait awhile, the impulse may weaken or die. Or, you can refer to this list when someone asks, "What do you want for your birthday, girl?"

| WAIT ITEM | PRICE TAG |
|---|---|
| | |
| | |
| | |
| | |
| | |

## Worth every shiny penny; soft soap and others

God do I love soft soap. It's actually a bit out of control. It's so much better than bar soap. It doesn't get stuck on your rings or leave a nasty mess in the sink. It doesn't slip out of your hands. It doesn't get hair stuck to it. And if you take into consideration the waste and extra clean-up of bar soap, it's cheaper! Other items that actually save you time, money and aggravation include rolling luggage, a wine recorker, a commuter mug, a grocery-bag trash can, etc. Make a list of stuff that could save you time and money.

| WORTHY ITEM | PRICE TAG | TIME/$$ SAVED |
|---|---|---|
| | | |
| | | |
| | | |
| | | |
| | | |

## Quit for one week

You can give up almost anything for one week. While I don't recommend it, my sister even quit food for a week, and she's still standing. Make a list of things you would consider giving up for one week. When the week is over, calculate how much time and money you saved. You may even decide to give up these things forever. My list includes TV, desserts, sugar, eating lunch out, soda and café coffee. I turned off the TV and saved enough time to write this little book!

QUIT ITEM                                    TIME/$$ SAVED

_____

_____

_____

_____

_____

_____

_____

_____

_____

## Your thrifty support group

Every thrifty girl needs a thrifty friend. I have my sister — she's *Frugal Girl*. I call her when I need a second opinion. We talked for hours (using unlimited weekend minutes) about my last condo purchase, discussing what I really needed in a home. How important is the view? How much space do I really need? Hey, it's great to bat these ideas around. I know what you're thinking. No, my sister isn't available — get your own friend! If it helps, make a *Thrifty Friends* list. Reconnect if you've lost touch.

_____

_____

_____

### ✦ THRIFTY TIPS ✦

**The value of education**
Everyone always thinks the more educated you are, the more money you will make. Try telling that to someone with a MFA in Ceramics. Please don't spend a bucket of money and hours of energy going back to school unless you know the value of the degree. Even an MBA might not be worth it! Everyone is always trying to get me to go back for my MFA. I always ask, "Why? So I can be an in-debt, overqualified artist?" Crunch the numbers, go to a cheaper school, attend a community college or skip the degree and take a few specialized classes. If time is money, school is more expensive than you ever thought.

**Net savings**
*Backache:* You don't need to cart your laptop to school. What? Did you think they were still using spiral notebooks?

**Take care**
It really pays to take care of your stuff. Don't abuse it! Treat it like it may be the last precious item you ever own — hang your clothes, change the oil and water the plants. Everything you don't have to replace saves you money.

**Net savings**
*Your time:* The longer things last, the less time you need to spend shopping.
*Rewashing:* No washing clothes that may or may not be dirty.
*Wheels:* Your car will last longer if you pamper it.
*Thousands:* Just think of the cash you'll save — start planning that vacation.

## The real estate bounty

These days, it's not that difficult to make good money on real estate. You don't have to invest in an apartment building and become a landlord or buy a fixer-upper and do a gut rehab to make a buck. I know plenty of folks who have managed to rake it in just by selling their own home. Some buy a place and sit on it 'til they're gray. Others start with a small place and trade up every few years.

Real estate is a good investment for many reasons. First, you get to live there. I'm sure you know the old, "paying rent is like throwing your money away" adage. There's some truth to it. Usually for a little more per month, you can own a home. Second, the interest you pay on your mortgage is tax deductible. And it's a great investment for girls who just aren't that good at socking money away. You don't want to lose your home. So, making mortgage payments is kind of like a mandatory savings plan. Finally, it's a fairly safe investment. There's no guarantee, but residential property tends to increase in value 5% or more every year.

So, I highly recommend buying a place to live — not a cavernous mansion, not a 400-acre ranch, not a downtown penthouse. You're trying to be thrifty, right? You want a place that's modest — modest price, modest square footage and modest neighborhood. Figure out what you need, get a good real estate agent, shop around and don't spend your last dime. If you're a first-time homebuyer, have low income or qualify for minority status, do research. There are lots of government programs to help.

## Money is paper

We move a lot of money around without actually thinking about its true value. Do you really think Martha Stewart thinks about money the same way you do? Of course not. She's probably carrying a $300 umbrella. Crap! I don't care if it keeps you stylishly dry!

So, how do you figure the value of something without dollar signs? Simple. Figure how much time it would take you to pay for something. If you make $8 an hour (after taxes), a $4 mocha just cost you 30 minutes of labor. Instead of looking at the $56 price tag, do the calculations and ask yourself, "Is this pair of jeans worth seven hours of MOI?" That really makes you think, doesn't it?

How much do you take home every week?        _____(a)

How many hours do you work a week?        _____(b)

Here's the math: $a \div b = c$

Here's what you make an hour:        _____(c)

---

### Chapter 7 homework: 2-12 minutes

If you don't own a home, take a minute to think about the kind of thrifty place you would purchase. Condo? House? Studio? One-bedroom? Square footage? Price? Money down? Location? View? Back yard? Parking? Garage?

_____

_____

_____

_____

_____

_____

_____

☐ Homework complete!

---

◆ THRIFTY TIPS ◆

**Ma wants a grandchild**
"I sympathize," from *The Diary of Thrifty Girl.* My mom wants one, too. You were not put on this planet to fulfill your parents' dreams. There's only one reason to have a child—YOU want one.

Have a kid or want one? I'll write a book for you. I'll call it *Thrifty Girl Goes Mommy.*

If children aren't in your future, tell Mom to get her own life! She's welcome to foster a child, volunteer at a daycare or work in a pediatric ward. Raising a child is no part-time job. When my mom said she'd like to have a grandchild, I smirked, looked at my two childless sisters and asked, "Have you considered adopting?"
**Net savings**
*Thousands of dollars:* You'll never have to buy diapers.
*Guilt:* You'll never think you're a bad mother.
*Aggravation:* You'll never hear, "When you were that age…"
*Taxi service:* You don't need to drive to soccer practice!

# 8

# THRIFTY IS FOREVER

Lovers come and go (speaking from experience), but thrifty is forever. It's all well and good to be thrifty for a month or two. The challenge is making thrifty last. In the beginning, you'll need to be diligent—thinking about every dollar you spend. After a little while, you'll get into a groove. You'll make a few little blunders here and there, but you'll get back on track. Finally, you'll get into a comfortable thrifty zone. You won't have to weigh every freakin' expenditure. Thrifty will just come naturally. I have all the confidence you can make the commitment.

Remember, Rome wasn't built in a day. You will repair your financial situation over time. The worse your situation is, the longer it will take. Try not to beat yourself up over past transgressions. Be diligent, be patient, reward yourself regularly and as Aunt Mary would say, "Finish your plate."

One last thing before I go. Naturally it's an incredibly long list of things to keep you thrifty forever ...

- ☐ Focus on the future
- ☐ Make sure you have the insurance you need
- ☐ Balance your checkbook
- ☐ Monitor your savings, investments and retirement
- ☐ Be diligent about your emergency fund
- ☐ Keep close tabs on your credit card debt
- ☐ Pay down your credit card debt
- ☐ Check your credit report yearly
- ☐ Stay healthy
- ☐ Get plenty of rest
- ☐ Take care of your things
- ☐ Know the difference between need and want
- ☐ Find a job you enjoy
- ☐ Save receipts
- ☐ Stay organized
- ☐ Put important dates on the calendar
- ☐ Find a thrifty significant other or remain single
- ☐ Invest in modest real estate
- ☐ Keep track of your short-term goals
- ☐ Stay focused on your long-term goals
- ☐ Value time as well as money
- ☐ Surround yourself with thrifty friends
- ☐ Appreciate the people in your life
- ☐ Don't compete with folks for material possessions
- ☐ Value quality over quantity
- ☐ Quit bad habits
- ☐ Keep your cash growing in interest-bearing accounts
- ☐ Keep track of your accomplishments
- ☐ Reward yourself regularly

Congratulations! Keep going, girl!

◆ THRIFTY TIPS ◆

**Please quit smoking**
Now is the time to quit. I admit I've never smoked—so I've never had to quit. I know it's hard. I've seen many folks through. If you take only one piece of advice from this book, quit smoking. It's killing you, your friends, and your significant other. It's even wrecking the environment. As if this weren't enough, it's costing you a fortune and making the fat tobacco MEN richer. Need help quitting? There are a ton of free programs on the web, just Google.

**Net savings**
*Your health:* What's worth more than your health?
*Piles of cash:* You'll save much more than one pile.
*Standing outside bars:* Eventually the law will prohibit you from smoking practically everywhere.

# EVERYTHING *you ever needed to know in one handy-dandy cluster o' charts*

YOUR SAVINGS

Keep track of savings here—checking, savings, emergency, #1 short-term goal, #1 long-term goal, the cash in your pocket—everything. Make a list under *savings*. Write the month by the *. Now, write the amount in the accounts under this month. Total. Do the same with investments and retirement accounts. Repeat monthly. There's enough room for 12 months!

| SAVINGS | * | | | | |
|---|---|---|---|---|---|
| | | | | | |
| | | | | | |
| | | | | | |
| | | | | | |
| | | | | | |
| TOTAL | | | | | |

| INVESTMENTS | * | | | | |
|---|---|---|---|---|---|
| | | | | | |
| | | | | | |
| | | | | | |
| TOTAL | | | | | |

| RETIREMENT | * | | | | |
|---|---|---|---|---|---|
| | | | | | |
| | | | | | |
| | | | | | |
| | | | | | |
| | | | | | |
| TOTAL | | | | | |

| ADD IT UP | * | | | | |
|---|---|---|---|---|---|
| SAVINGS | | | | | |
| INVESTMENTS | | | | | |
| RETIREMENT | | | | | |
| GRAND TOTAL | | | | | |

| | | | | | | |
|---|---|---|---|---|---|---|
| | | | | | | |
| | | | | | | |
| | | | | | | |
| | | | | | | |
| | | | | | | |
| | | | | | | |

| | | | | | | |
|---|---|---|---|---|---|---|
| | | | | | | |
| | | | | | | |
| | | | | | | |
| | | | | | | |

| | | | | | | |
|---|---|---|---|---|---|---|
| | | | | | | |
| | | | | | | |
| | | | | | | |
| | | | | | | |
| | | | | | | |
| | | | | | | |

| | | | | | | |
|---|---|---|---|---|---|---|
| | | | | | | |
| | | | | | | |
| | | | | | | |
| | | | | | | |

## YOUR DEBT

Over here, you're going to track your debt—credit card, student loan, car loan, etc. List them all under *debt*. Don't put your mortgage here—list that in OTHER STUFF on page 52. Again, put this month by the * and give it all a grand total. Don't get depressed. It's just a number. Repeat monthly. There's enough room for 12 months!

| DEBT | * | | | | |
|------|---|---|---|---|---|
| | | | | | |
| | | | | | |
| | | | | | |
| | | | | | |
| | | | | | |
| | | | | | |
| | | | | | |
| | | | | | |
| | | | | | |
| | | | | | |
| | | | | | |
| | | | | | |
| GRAND TOTAL | | | | | |

## YOUR NET WORTH

Now let's take a look at the bottom line. Again with this month by the *. Put the *grand total* from page 48 in the + TOTAL row and the *grand total* from debt on this page in the  - TOTAL row. Subtract - TOTAL from + TOTAL and write it in NET TOTAL. If your debt is greater than your savings, the number will be negative. Take a deep breath. Repeat monthly.

| NET WORTH | * | | | | |
|-----------|---|---|---|---|---|
| + TOTAL | | | | | |
| - TOTAL | | | | | |
| NET TOTAL | | | | | |

|  |  |  |  |  |  |  |
|---|---|---|---|---|---|---|
|  |  |  |  |  |  |  |
|  |  |  |  |  |  |  |
|  |  |  |  |  |  |  |
|  |  |  |  |  |  |  |
|  |  |  |  |  |  |  |
|  |  |  |  |  |  |  |
|  |  |  |  |  |  |  |
|  |  |  |  |  |  |  |
|  |  |  |  |  |  |  |
|  |  |  |  |  |  |  |
|  |  |  |  |  |  |  |
|  |  |  |  |  |  |  |
|  |  |  |  |  |  |  |
|  |  |  |  |  |  |  |

|  |  |  |  |  |  |  |
|---|---|---|---|---|---|---|
|  |  |  |  |  |  |  |
|  |  |  |  |  |  |  |
|  |  |  |  |  |  |  |

## OTHER STUFF *you might want to track*

This is the place to track anything that's not covered elsewhere—how much you made this month, the balance on your mortgage, how much your house/condo is worth, how much you charged on your credit card, etc. You decide what you want to track.

| OTHER STUFF | * | | | | |
|---|---|---|---|---|---|
| | | | | | |
| | | | | | |
| | | | | | |
| | | | | | |
| | | | | | |
| | | | | | |
| | | | | | |
| | | | | | |
| | | | | | |
| | | | | | |
| | | | | | |
| | | | | | |
| | | | | | |
| | | | | | |
| | | | | | |
| | | | | | |
| | | | | | |
| | | | | | |
| | | | | | |
| | | | | | |
| | | | | | |
| | | | | | |
| | | | | | |
| | | | | | |
| | | | | | |
| | | | | | |
| | | | | | |
| | | | | | |
| | | | | | |

|  |  |  |  |  |  |  |
|---|---|---|---|---|---|---|
|  |  |  |  |  |  |  |
|  |  |  |  |  |  |  |
|  |  |  |  |  |  |  |
|  |  |  |  |  |  |  |
|  |  |  |  |  |  |  |
|  |  |  |  |  |  |  |
|  |  |  |  |  |  |  |
|  |  |  |  |  |  |  |
|  |  |  |  |  |  |  |
|  |  |  |  |  |  |  |
|  |  |  |  |  |  |  |
|  |  |  |  |  |  |  |
|  |  |  |  |  |  |  |
|  |  |  |  |  |  |  |
|  |  |  |  |  |  |  |
|  |  |  |  |  |  |  |
|  |  |  |  |  |  |  |
|  |  |  |  |  |  |  |
|  |  |  |  |  |  |  |
|  |  |  |  |  |  |  |
|  |  |  |  |  |  |  |
|  |  |  |  |  |  |  |
|  |  |  |  |  |  |  |
|  |  |  |  |  |  |  |
|  |  |  |  |  |  |  |
|  |  |  |  |  |  |  |
|  |  |  |  |  |  |  |
|  |  |  |  |  |  |  |
|  |  |  |  |  |  |  |
|  |  |  |  |  |  |  |
|  |  |  |  |  |  |  |
|  |  |  |  |  |  |  |
|  |  |  |  |  |  |  |

# What it's costing

Daily/ 365 times a year

| $1 per day is | $365 year and about | $4700 after 10 years at 5% interest |
|---|---|---|
| $2 | $730 | $9400 |
| $3 | $1095 | $14100 |
| $4 | $1460 | $18800 |
| $5 | $1825 | $23500 |
| $6 | $2190 | $28200 |
| $7 | $2555 | $32900 |
| $8 | $2920 | $37600 |
| $9 | $3285 | $42300 |
| $10 | $3650 | $47000 |

So, if you skip your daily mocha ($4) and put that money in the bank at 5%, you'd have about $18,800 after 10 years. That should wake you up!

Weekly/52 times a year

| $1 per week is | $52 year and about | $665 after 10 years at 5% interest |
|---|---|---|
| $2 | $104 | $1330 |
| $3 | $156 | $1995 |
| $4 | $208 | $2660 |
| $5 | $260 | $3325 |
| $6 | $312 | $3980 |
| $7 | $364 | $4655 |
| $8 | $416 | $5320 |
| $9 | $468 | $5985 |
| $10 | $520 | $6650 |
| $15 | $780 | $9975 |
| $20 | $1040 | $13300 |
| $25 | $1300 | $16625 |

So, if you cut back on dining out ($20) and put that money in the bank at 5%, you'd have about $13,300 after 10 years. You could put that toward a hybrid car and save even more!

Monthly/12 times a year

| $5 per month is | $60 a year and about | $790 after 10 years at 5% interest |
|---|---|---|
| $10 | $120 | $1580 |
| $15 | $180 | $2370 |
| $20 | $240 | $3160 |
| $25 | $300 | $3950 |
| $30 | $360 | $4740 |
| $35 | $420 | $5530 |
| $40 | $480 | $6320 |
| $50 | $600 | $7900 |

So, if you can reduce your rent ($50) and put that money in the bank at 5%, you'd have about $7,900 after 10 years. You'll probably buy your own place before 10 years is up!

## *Alexis Steinkamp is* THRIFTY GIRL

**I'm not an uptight financial guru; I'm just a thrifty girl!**
I'm not an accountant, financial planner or even a math wiz, but my friends call me *Thrifty Girl*. Believe me, I've been called worse. They're amazed that I make less money than they do and have something to show for it! Look, I'm an artist and I've never made a ton of money. You should have seen the jaws drop when I told my friends I was buying my first condo. A couple years ago, my annual income was less than $10,000! I haven't suffered irreversible damage. Instead, I paid off a truckload of student loans, traveled the globe and purchased a condo—all without turning tricks, living off a 69-year-old sugar daddy, selling crack or maxing out my cards. How? Simple—by being thrifty.

But I don't just sit around all day sipping chardonnay and counting my nickels. I have a day job. I'm a graphic designer at Truman College in Chicago, where I also teach classes in web design. When I'm not at Truman or thinking about thrift, I'm curled up on my sofa in my studio condo watching a movie, or behind a vodka gimlet with friends at the Green Mill.